A Collection of Poems

A.E. Lee

Copyright © 2023 A.E. Lee
All rights reserved
First Edition

Fulton Books
Meadville, PA

Published by Fulton Books 2023

ISBN 979-8-88731-039-8 (paperback)
ISBN 979-8-88731-040-4 (digital)

Printed in the United States of America

To Ley

Contents

Introduction ix

Seeking Solace
    The Dragonfly 3
    The Message of the Blue Heron 4
    By Grace 5
    Silence Is an Answer 6
    The Light at the End 7
    And Now We Heal 8
    Her Voice 9
    Angel Above 11
    Let the Waves Carry You 12
    Mistakes 13
    Space and Time 14
    You Are Safe 15
    Celebrate Life 17
    The Willow Tree 18
    The Universe Will Protect You 19
    Go Look at the Moon 20
    Becoming a Butterfly 21
    This or Something Better 22
    Overcoming the Fear Within 23
    You've Got This 24
    Survivor 25

Seeking Gratitude
    Here's to the Women 29
    My City 30
    My Son, My Moon, My Stars 31

Thank Heavens for Little Girls 33
Where Has the Time Gone? 35
Go Thank a Teacher 36
I Am Lucky 37
Thank You, More Please 38
Motherhood 39
To My True Partner in Crime 41

Seeking Inspiration
Eat the Cake 45
New Year 47
Worth the Wait 48
Be a Unicorn 49
Heart Sing 51
Love the Sky You're Under 52
Champagne Wishes 53
Finding Your Purpose 54
The Power of Pink 55
Spring Flower 56
Inhale Peace, Exhale Joy 57
Let's Have an Adventure 58
Courage and Kindness 59
Worthy of Love 60
Baseball Is Life 62
Daisy 63
Pump Your Legs and Swing 64
Lapis Lazuli 65
Turn the Page 67

Seeking Love
To Find Your Person 71
Bewitched 72
All In 73
Thinking of You 74
Whose Hands Are Whose 75

Today, Tomorrow, Always 76
The Air I Breathe 77
Soul to Soul 78
You Can Lean on Me 79

Acknowledgments 81

Introduction

    I hate writing poetry—dread it, actually. As a sixth-grade teacher, I always hated our unit on poetry. And then, all of the sudden, while on a train to New York City, something magical happened: I wrote a poem for a dear friend's wedding. It just came to me, and I started typing. I loved it instantly, and when I eventually gave it to her, she did too.

    I thought it was a fluke, a one-time thing. Then, one Saturday morning I was asked to write something for another wedding. As I was taking notes about the couple, I began to form the poem in my head. I put the phone down and ran to my computer to type.

    After I finished that poem, another one came to me. Then another one. Then another one. And so on. I decided to take on a challenge of writing sixty poems in sixty days. I completed it, finishing the poems well within the sixty-day time frame.

    Writing these poems is what I turned to when I was seeking something—solace, gratitude, inspiration, and love. I divided this book into those four sections for that reason. My hope is that whatever you may be seeking, you will find a source of comfort through these poems, as I have.

    Thank you for reading. Here's to loving poetry!

Seeking Solace

The Dragonfly

I am with you, I am always with you—
from the moment you met, I was there
fluttering my iridescent wings.

I am with you, I am always with you—
on the beach in May
where you took your first steps as Husband and Wife.

I am with you, I am always with you—
as you dance your first dance
twirling around those in person and spirit whom you love.

I am with you, I am always with you—
in dreams and life,
sending you hope and love.

I am with you, I am always with you—
reminding you to live life to its fullest,
to live in the moment.

The dragonfly's greatest gift is to remind as
all to live our lives without regret.
And to remind you that I am with you, I am always with you.

The Message of the Blue Heron

The long thin legs of the heron
Pleading with us to stand on our own

Choose to soar

Innate wisdom to maneuver through life
Inspiring all to cocreate our own circumstances

Choose to soar

Walking slowly…standing…waiting
Trusting all will come at the right time

Choose to soar

Exuding a graceful energy
Offering peace and serenity

Choose to soar

Following its own unique path
Encouraging us to follow ours

Choose to soar

Embracing the flaws
Love your whole self
Choose to soar

By Grace

Alluring
with a mischievous sense of humor—
beguiled by Grace.

Glint of naughtiness in her eyes
was never lost—
beguiled by Grace.

Devastatingly beautiful,
an untouchable version of ourselves—
beguiled by Grace.

The most intriguing creature,
and regal to match—
beguiled by Grace.

Vibrant with life,
but dying in the moonlight—
beguiled by Grace

Born from a city of love,
with family at the heart—
beguiled by Grace.

Silence Is an Answer

In the stillness of the night,
the quiet is deafening.
Silence is an answer, too.

We say goodbye,
without a spoken word.
Silence is an answer, too.

The heartbeats of two, no longer in sync.
dreams become scarce.
Silence is an answer, too.

A hush of a beloved voice
is as good an answer as words.
Silence is an answer, too.

Not getting what you thought you wanted
can be a wonderful stroke of luck.
Silence is an answer, too.

Searching for something that can't be reached,
you must shut the door.
Silence is an answer, too.

The Light at the End

It may be dim at first—
do not fear the darkness.
There is light.

A metaphor for hope,
understand what awaits.
There is light.

Use the suffering
as fuel to battle.
There is light.

The illumination is your life,
and a tunnel is temporary.
There is light.

Storms do not last,
so keep fighting.
There is light.

Crawl through the blackness.
believe you are nearing the end.
There is light.

And Now We Heal

See my scars.
You can rebuild.
(And now we heal.)

Acknowledge your wounds.
Be brave.
(And now we heal.)

The hurt will fade.
You will be free once more.
(And now we heal.)

Everyone collapses.
But then we rise.
(And now we heal.)

You are not without hope.
The power lies within.
(And now we heal.)

Do not speed up the clock.
Rediscover the beauty in time.
(And now we heal.)

Her Voice

Remembering her voice—
etched in your heart,
deep within the soul.

Remembering her voice—
echoed in all you do,
still within your daily thoughts.

Remembering her voice—
the laughter, walks,
talking for hours.

Remembering her voice—
signs all around
that she is still here.

Remembering her voice—
long after she is gone,
urging to remember who you are.

Remembering her voice—
memories stretched thin with time
Still visited when you feel lost.

Angel Above

Dancing with the clouds
Hearing the whispers of love
Angel above

The message of comfort,
During this transformative time
Angel above

My guardian, my guide—
Wrapping me in protection and healing
Angel above

Reminding me to rest
They've got me covered
Angel above

Imploring me to let go
Allowing myself to be wrapped in their wings
Angel above

The divine opening of my eyes
Engulfing me with warmth
Angel above

Let the Waves Carry You

Have faith
where the light cannot reach—
let the waves carry you.

Stop running
and allow the ocean to come—
let the waves carry you.

Learn to ride it out
as it's useless to try and stop—
let the waves carry you.

Find your true direction
by learning how to surf—
let the waves carry you.

Don't push the sea away
as it will always come back to shore—
let the waves carry you.

Dance with the saltwater,
and permit the music of the sea to set you free—
let the waves carry you.

Mistakes

Making mistakes does not make you bad—
it makes you human.
It's okay, everyone makes mistakes.

Do not be afraid—
part of living is making them.
It's okay, everyone makes mistakes.

You are here,
and you have the power to shape tomorrow.
It's okay, everyone makes mistakes.

Learn from them,
don't let your struggles be in vain.
It's okay, everyone makes mistakes.

Create the power in you
to be a better version of yourself.
It's okay, everyone makes mistakes.

This does not define you;
how you correct the past does.
It's okay, everyone makes mistakes.

Space and Time

Space and time are not the enemy:

They are essential
to overcome any obstacle and heal the heart;

The frame of our present universe,
imperative in accomplishing anything in this world;

A creation for ourselves—
to recover, think, and just be;

Meant for us,
forces that cannot be destroyed;

Love from a distance,
to get one's mind precise.

For without space,
there is no time.

You Are Safe

You become your true self
when you realize your comfort comes from within.

You
are
safe.

Safe is a feeling;
a belief that cannot be invented.

You
are
safe.

Overcome the darkness
that threatens to swallow you whole.

You
are
safe.

Dive into your wounds,
expose and release your shadows.

You
are
safe.

Know you can sink your head into the pillow
and wake with the promise of a new day.

You
are
safe.

Be your own safe space;
it will evolve as you become who you are meant to be.

You
are
safe.

Celebrate Life

Life is what you toast
even at its end—
celebrate life!

Remembering the best times
and the laughter—
celebrate life!

The more you celebrate your life,
the more there is to celebrate—
celebrate life!

Life should not just be lived.
it should be celebrated—
celebrate life!

Remember the milestones,
as well as the road ahead—
celebrate life!

Don't wait for the special occasion;
find a reason every day—
celebrate life!

The Willow Tree

The goddess tree
Endurance in challenging times
Survive, strength, grow

Wisdom, power, grace: the willow
The calm in the chaos
Survive, strength, grow

Let go of the pain and suffering
Be newer, stronger, bolder
Survive, strength, grow

Thrive with the water
A deep inner knowledge
Survive, strength, grow

Tree of immortality
Breathing in new life through its branches
Survive, strength, grow

Stabilizing force
Beloved tree
Survive, strength, grow

The Universe Will Protect You

Be brave and let go—
there is a beautiful plan for you,
and the universe will protect you.

Many blessings are in store for you,
so trust and surrender,
and the universe will protect you.

Everything is unfolding,
exactly when and how it is meant to be,
and the universe will protect you.

Please do not worry;
it will do what it wills.
And the universe will protect you.

When dreams die,
another one gently takes its place.
And the universe will protect you.

Believe that your journey
will take you beyond your heart's desires,
and the universe will protect you.

Go Look at the Moon

Someone, somewhere
is gazing up too.
Go look at the moon.

Glance up
and see the most romantic spot in our universe.
Go look at the moon.

The moon stares back
and sparkles through the darkness.
Go look at the moon.

The moon is always there,
even in a thick blanket of clouds.
Go look at the moon.

See the inspiration from the moonlight,
even when you feel far from full.
Go look at the moon.

Like you, it shines brightly,
even when no one is able to see it.
Go look at the moon.

Becoming a Butterfly

Butterflies
remind us what a gift it is to be alive

Delighting in its beauty
Appreciating the change it had to achieve

Growing, as the caterpillar goes through its process
(Give yourself time)

You must want to fly so much
that you are willing to give all of yourself

Open your heart and mind
this change just might give you wings

And when the world feels as it is ending,
You transform into your true self

Become a butterfly

This or Something Better

Breathe in the amazing
Exhale through the awful
...this or something better

It is not rejection
But redirection for a higher purpose
...this or something better

Let go of what you thought you wanted
Only then will something greater come
...this or something better

Everything happens for a reason
Stay present, stay patient
...this or something better

Draw in what you expect
Become what you respect
...this or something better

When you least expect it
Something far superior will appear
...this or something better

Overcoming the Fear Within

Thinking will not overcome the fear within—
only action will.
Lean into the fear.

Nothing more than the story within us—
write a new chapter.
Lean into the fear.

Do not let your anxiety of what-if
keep anything from happening.
Lean into the fear.

Have your decisions reflect your hopes—
not your trepidations.
Lean into the fear.

Your heart's desire
is on the other side of this angst.
Lean into the fear.

Take one small step forward
and you just might soar.
Lean into the fear.

You've Got This

Learn to dance in the rain,
or the storm may never pass.

You already have what it takes,
so believe in your own potential.

You've got this.

The mountains you climb will not be easy,
but the view from the top will be worth it

Inhale the good vibes
and exhale the bad.

You've got this.

No one has your back
like you do.

You have two choices:
give up or get up.

You've got this.

Survivor

You are stronger
than what tried to break you—
this does not define you

The strength of your spirit tested,
you had no choice—
this does not define you

Powerful and capable,
you must keep going—
this does not define you

Remember, after the rain
the skies always clear—
this does not define you.

You can make it through,
Because you are a warrior—
You are not what happened—
You are what you choose to become—
This *does* define you

Seeking Gratitude

Here's to the Women

Here's to the women!
You are a queen
Your soul is majestic

Here's to the women!
You can be unstoppable
Once you find your voice

Here's to the women!
Every time you stand up
You stand up for us all
The fire inside you
Is stronger than what surrounds you

Here's to the women!
If you fall
You will rise up stronger than before

Here's to the women!
To those who came before us
And to those who have just begun

My City

City of Brotherly Love,
my forever home:
Philadelphia.

A true character,
you have to have guts to succeed there:
Philadelphia

Longing for the "wooder" ice—
only after my "wit wiz" cheese steak:
Philadelphia.

Getting jimmies…not sprinkles
down the shore:
Philadelphia.

From Broad to South,
Rocky to Royalty:
Philadelphia.

A state of mind
I'm always in:
Philadelphia.

My Son, My Moon, My Stars

There is nothing quite like the bond between a mother and her son.
        My son,
           my moon,
             my stars.

As I look into your eyes, I am thankful for such a miracle.
        My son,
           my moon,
             my stars.

My love for you will help you grow stronger, not weaker.
        My son,
           my moon,
             my stars.

I admire your tender heart and cherish your laugh.
        My son,
           my moon,
             my stars

You stole my heart the minute you were first placed in my arms.
My son,
my moon,
my stars.

I learned the definition of true love when I met my beautiful boy.
My son,
my moon,
my stars.

Thank Heavens for Little Girls

My heart,
my soul,
the best thing I ever made.
Thank heaven for little girls.

The source of many laughs,
and a few tears,
she is simply my world.
Thank heaven for little girls.

Giving me reason
to always keep going,
to never give up.
Thank heaven for little girls.

Rejoicing
in her infectious laugh—
she is only this little once.
Thank heaven for little girls.

The world has been waiting
for such a joyous,
spirited soul.
Thank heaven for little girls.

For all the hands
I have ever held,
hers are by far the best.
Thank heaven for little girls.

Where Has the Time Gone?

The days are endless,
and the years pass in a blink.
Where has the time gone?

It was just yesterday
that you took your first breath in my arms.
Where has the time gone?

You're a piece of me living on the outside,
one of the few to know my heartbeat from within.
Where has the time gone?

The little feet and hands won't stay little,
so enjoy every moment.
Where has the time gone?

Not just you have grown—
I have, too.
Where has the time gone?

Go Thank a Teacher

The best lessons are not learned in books,
but are learned from the heart.
For that, go thank a teacher.

Inspiration to be better,
carried wherever we go.
For that, go thank a teacher.

The compass that guides
a lifelong love of learning.
For that, go thank a teacher.

Awakening our sense of self,
and empowering us to chase our dreams.
For that, go thank a teacher.

Much like a candle,
lighting the way for others.
For that, go thank a teacher.

Protector,
Stand-in parent,
Friend.
Thank you, teacher.

I Am Lucky

The blessings that occur
Regardless of your means:
This is luck

Feeling fortunate
In your heart and mind:
This is luck

Taking what the world throws
Not letting it get you down:
This is luck

The serendipity
Of not getting what you want:
This is luck

Take the time to inhale
Take in life's miracles:
This is luck

Appreciation of life's fate
Never taking it for granted:
This is luck

Thank You, More Please

With gratitude, the universe is abundant.
Thank you, more please.

Appreciate life's gifts, and believe they are yours to have.
Thank you, more please.

Draw in more of what makes you happy
and open doors to your dreams.
Thank you, more please.

New beginnings, and the ability to see life's lessons in the old—
Thank you, more please.

All the I love yous, and the gift of time to say the final farewell.
Thank you, more please.

If it's said often with devotion, watch miracles unfold—

Motherhood

Momma, Mommy, Mom
(saint, hero, superwoman)
Being a mom isn't easy.

Sleepless nights, constant worrying, endless to do list
(putting their needs before your own)
Being a mom isn't easy.

They do not need perfection
(just you)
Being a mom isn't easy.

Try your best
(never give up, despite the struggle)
Being a mom isn't easy.

No one could love them more
(not a soul)
Being a mom isn't easy.

It is the most rewarding sacrifice
(from their first breath until your last)
Being a mom isn't easy.

To My True Partner in Crime

Someone to have fun with
In chorus, at the beach, sitting on the couch
A true partner in crime

Someone you trust
Secrets, lies, and the college years
A true partner in crime

Someone you confide in
Love, loss, and everything in between
A true partner in crime

Someone who knows you
Better than you know yourself
A true partner in crime

Someone you can count on for a lifetime
A best friend
A true partner in crime

Seeking Inspiration

Eat the Cake

With their dying breath,
no one regrets one last piece—
Eat the Cake.

Take the vacation,
and lean into the warmth of the sun—
Eat the Cake.

Partake in the night out,
laugh too loud and drink too much—
Eat the Cake.

Buy the outfit, feel like yourself again,
You. Are. Beautiful.
Eat the Cake.

Find your passion
and feed your soul
Eat the Cake.

Tomorrow is guaranteed to no one
so live as if each day is your last.
Eat the Cake.

New Year

A prayer, not a resolution
As a blank chapter stands

Take the leap of faith
Look at the potential, rather than the flaws

What the new year becomes
Relies on what you bring

It's the magic of new beginnings

A potent reminder that some of our best days
Are yet to come

And that you still have yet to meet
All who will love you

We are here, let's make it our own
Tomorrow is not promised

It's the magic of new beginnings.

Worth the Wait

You are not behind.

The place you are now
Is where you are meant to be.

There is no set timetable
To find your passion.

One day
Your life's puzzle will be complete.

Do not change or alter
Your journey to fit another's.

You will get where you want to be
Thankful you took your time

The best things in life
Are worth the wait.

Be a Unicorn

Swim with mermaids
Chase rainbows
Don't hide your magic
Believe in yourself

Be a unicorn

Enjoy your life's journey
Trust in miracles

Embrace your individuality
Sparkle from within
Be a unicorn

You are unbreakable and unique
Brave, beautiful, and kind

If you believe in me
I'll believe in you

Be a unicorn.

Heart Sing

Dare to give your life expression
To your soul's desire:
Something to make your heart sing

Discover what makes your eyes sparkle
What brings out your smile:
Something to make your heart sing

Create your own music
Always make it apart of your life:
Something to make your heart sing

Trust your gut
Nourish your inspiration:
Something to make your heart sing

Spread your joy
Make your happiness a priority:
Something to make your heart sing

Find your passion
Design the best vision of your life:
Something to make your heart sing

Love the Sky You're Under

It's where you belong
It's where you are meant to be
Love the sky you're under

Fall in love with your journey
While letting go of your past
Love the sky you're under

Stop comparing your sky to someone else's
It's yours for a reason
Love the sky you're under

Look up to the vastness
Appreciate you are here now for a purpose
Love the sky you're under

Lean into the beauty of the unknown
Millions of stars await your discovery
Love the sky you're under

It's where you belong
It's where you are meant to be
Love the sky you're under

Champagne Wishes

A wish for you: cheers in the bad times, just as much as in the good.
have a glass…or two…or three.
Champagne can solve the problem.

There is no such thing as too much—
sometimes it's the only thing that helps.
Champagne can solve the problem

Take in the characteristics of your favorite pour:
be bright, glittery, bubbly.
Champagne can solve the problem.

Taste the stars—be the first to toast and the last to bid farewell.
throw confetti and greet the coming of a new day with a smile
Champagne can solve the problem.

Finding Your Purpose

To find your purpose
First you must locate your wounds
Your purpose will set you free

The heart begins a new rhythm
When you discover what absorbs your being
Your purpose will set you free

It is why you were put on this earth
And how you truly come alive
Your purpose will set you free

The true meaning of this life
Is to make a difference
Your purpose will set you free

Unearth your gift
Then give it away to the world
Your purpose will set you free

You will know without a doubt
It will transform you into your most powerful self
Your purpose will set you free

The Power of Pink

All words have color,
and some help you shine brighter than others, but
Pink is my signature color.

A little…or a lot…
just the thought makes me smile!
Pink is my signature color.

Straddling red and white, and
leaving us with the hue of unconditional love.
Pink is my signature color.

The color of strength and compassion, it
makes everything more beautiful than before.
Pink is my signature color.

The shade the sun makes
when it kisses the twilight sky.
Pink is my signature color.

If we believe in the power of pink, then
the world will be a better place.
Pink is my signature color.

Spring Flower

Where the flowers open,
so does hope.
(You are a spring flower.)

There will always be more springtide,
this year and next.
(You are a spring flower.)

Shimmer in the present,
never look ahead.
(You are a spring flower.)

Despite the forecast,
live like it is always May.
(You are a spring flower.)

When nature resumes her brilliancy,
so does the human soul.
(You are a spring flower.)

May you grow and blossom
As the vibrant bloom you are—
(You are a spring flower.)

Inhale Peace, Exhale Joy

Simply by breathing,
you can bring your mind home once more.
Inhale peace, exhale joy.

Close your eyes,
breathe deep.
Inhale peace, exhale joy.

Still your imagination,
let go of stress and worry.
Inhale peace, exhale joy.

Do not let your anxiety break you—
breathe and practice silence.
Inhale peace, exhale joy.

Be tranquil and beautiful,
blow out the old and useless.
Inhale peace, exhale joy.

Embrace the calm
and just be.
Inhale peace, exhale joy.

Let's Have an Adventure

Sometimes the best plan
is to not have one at all—
let's have an adventure, shall we?

Let's trust and let go
and see what happens—
let's have adventure, shall we?

We'll have a good look at the world
before night's darkness sets in—
let's have an adventure, shall we?

Follow our hearts
and let wanderlust unfold—
let's have an adventure, shall we?

Let our feats take us further
than our fears ever could—
let's have an adventure, shall we?

We should dare to dream
and love our life to its fullest—
let's have an adventure, shall we?

Courage and Kindness

Have courage and be kind
In the absence of courage
No other goodness can appear

Have courage and be kind
Be brave enough to stand alone
And walk through the fear

Have courage and be kind
Even when you cannot control the outcome
Show up and be compassionate

Have courage and be kind
Where there is kindness and compassion
Magic can still be found

Have courage and be kind
Be fearless and selfless
Help those whose battles are unknown

Courage and kindness
Is a language all can speak

Worthy of Love

You are worthy of being chosen,
of being fought for—
you are worthy of love.

You are remarkable, and
no storm can take that away—
you are worthy of love.

You and all your layers are not a burden,
so hold that close—
you are worthy of love.

You are a living gift,
so embrace your inner beauty—
you are worthy of love.

You are capable of greatness,
and deserve to be cherished and adored—
you are worthy of love.

You are entitled to it all,
and must do whatever it takes to create it for yourself—
you are worthy of love.

Baseball Is Life

The smell of a warm spring breeze
The sound of the ball colliding with the bat

As the ball comes closer
it reminds you to be ready for anything—

No matter your age or size, you can flourish

Don't let your fear cause you to strike out

Worry over what can't be controlled is wasted, on and off the field

That's the beautiful thing about baseball—
If you give it your all, you never truly lose

Daisy

Sweet daisy—
the flower with the most pleasing smell,
simple and pure.

Sweet daisy—
when spring awakens
it gives us all stardust.

Sweet daisy—
a symbol of new beginnings,
and our ability to transform.

Sweet daisy—
Sprinkled here on Earth,
for all to stare and wonder.

Sweet daisy—
like sunshine on the ground.
not letting anyone get trampled…not even you.

Sweet daisy—
reminds us of how we are all connected, much like the stars above.

Pump Your Legs and Swing

Swing out—
dance, sing, laugh, have fun—
pump your legs and swing

May your toes touch the sky—
and may you fly without wings—
pump your legs and swing

Your life will continue to swing—
backward and forward—
pump your legs and swing

The higher you swing,
the harder it will be to fall—
pump your legs and swing

But if you do fall off,
just get back up and sway—
pump your legs and swing

Your dreams are within reach—
Just. Keep. Swinging.

Lapis Lazuli

The beautiful blue stone

Symbolic of wisdom and strength
Combining the blues of the heavens
And the glittery gold of the sun

Lapis Lazuli

The oldest and most revered jewel
Worn by ancient royalty
The stone of the Virgin Mary
Bringing inner peace and hope

Lapis Lazuli

Boosting the self-awareness
While strengthening the spiritual connection
Helping all to speak
One's deepest inner truth

Lapis Lazuli

Turn the Page

Life is one great novel
(some chapters are happy…some are challenging)—
Turn the page, write a new chapter.

Move on from the sad sections
(they are in the past for a reason)—
Turn the page, write a new chapter.

Keep reading
(don't close the whole book)—
Turn the page, write a new chapter.

Let the next story begin
(right now, right here)—
Turn the page, write a new chapter.

There's more to your novel
(more than the page you are stuck on)—
Turn the page, write a new chapter.

This is how bad stories end
(and the best stories begin!)—
Turn the page, write a new chapter.

Seeking Love

To Find Your Person

The Greeks believed we were cut in half
Destined to wander the earth
Looking for our person

Wandering the earth
Until we find the one our being has known since first glance and
we may have found our person

It just "clicks" and
when we are apart an unexplainable hole appears
This could be our person

Looking down
Wondering whose hands are whose
We want this to be our person

Promises, hopes, and dreams
Our soul's recognition of itself in another
We have found our person

As you say your vows on this day
we signal to the earth
This is my person.

Bewitched

The whole world fell in love one night
Hearts went under lock and key
Gleefully, enchantingly, bewitched

Under the sleepless night sky
Love came and told me not to slumber
Gleefully, enchantingly, bewitched

Longing for the day
To cling to one another
Gleefully, enchantingly, bewitched

Charmed
Now transfixed, unable to breath
Gleefully, enchantingly, bewitched

Our wild little secret
We still long for the universe to hear
Gleefully, enchantingly, bewitched

Enamored and transformed
A spell has been cast
Gleefully, enchantingly, bewitched

All In

I will love you—
when life appears messy,
and darkness seeps in.

I will love you—
when your past comes back to haunt you,
and your future seems so distant.

I will love you—
when your accomplishments sparkle.
and your mistakes darken.

I will love you—
when you are hurting,
and feel broken.

I will love you—
when you shimmer so brightly.
and your heart is light with laughter.

For as long as we are one,
never a question or wonder—
I will love you—always.

Thinking of You

In my mind
Or in my heart
I think of you

I keep myself busy
But when I pause
I think of you

In the morning, midday, and at night
Every moment
I think of you

Between yesterday, tomorrow, and today
It is always you
I think of

When I want to feel happiness
I just close my eyes
I think of you

With you occupying my mind
Holding the key to everything
I think of you

Whose Hands Are Whose

The first time we touched
My heart beats faster with every passing minute
Whose hands are whose

I look down
Unable to distinguish his fingers from my own
Whose hands are whose

As he held my face in his hands
I fell in love
Whose hands are whose

A steady hand
Reassuring that he will keep my heart safe
Whose hands are whose

Hopeful he will never let go
Allowing our love to grow over this lifetime into the next
Whose hands are whose

I knew in that moment
He was my home
Whose hands are whose

Today, Tomorrow, Always

I never knew what love felt like
Until you
Today, tomorrow, and always

Hand in hand
By my side
Today, tomorrow, and always

Falling in love
Again and again
Today, tomorrow, and always

Just us two
For the rest of our lives
Today, tomorrow, and always

For always
In all ways
Today, tomorrow, and always

I will love you today
I will love you tomorrow
I will love you always

The Air I Breathe

The thought of you wakes me each morning
And is what I fall asleep to each night
You are the air I breathe

Exhaling and then
Making room for our love
You are the air I breathe

The air you breathe in is the same as mine
Connecting us by love
You are the air I breathe

You are my universe
You are everything I need
You are the air I breathe

The language we speak
The promises we make
You are the air I breathe

Visions of you dance in my head
My heart sings along
You are the air I breathe

Soul to Soul

I recognized you instantly
Our souls already knew one another
Soul to soul

I felt a pull
Unlike any felt before
Soul to soul

It is our profound connection
That stopped us both to feel more
Soul to soul

Even when our voices are silent
Our souls speak their deep language
Soul to soul

Well worn, but wise
We meet in the middle of each of our stories
Soul to soul

It was the desire to know our own souls
That led us to one another
Soul to soul

You Can Lean on Me

We'll be okay—
I'll lean on you and
you can lean on me

I can promise you:
you won't face your obstacles alone and
you can lean on me

I will fall with you—
and pick you back up—
you can lean on me.

The only four words you need:
I'm here for you.
you can lean on me.

A hand for you to hold, and
an ear to listen—
you can lean on me.

Knowing what it is like to have no one,
allows me to be someone for you—
you can lean on me.

Acknowledgments

Thank you to everyone at Fulton Books for taking care of my work as if it were their own words. Words will never be able to express my gratitude to everyone who has made this possible.

Thank you to my editor, Megan Zavala, who once again helped to turn my words into a beautiful work of art that I am so proud to share with you.

My beautiful family and friends, the support that you show me day in and day out (especially on this new journey) is so humbling. I am eternally grateful for each and every one of you.

Ethan and Tessa, my constant inspiration. Everything I do is for you, because of you.

And to all of you, thank you for once again picking up my work. I hope that I once again was able to inspire you.

About the Author

A.E. Lee started her career in Pennsylvania politics, and while she had hoped it would be everything like her favorite TV show *The West Wing*, she quickly learned it was not. Long hours, little pay, and even less respect—she decided it was time for a change and embarked on a second career in education. She is now a beloved sixth-grade teacher in Fairfax County, Virginia.

She resides there now with her two beautiful children, Ethan and Tessa, where she continues her passion for writing and being a domestic violence advocate.

CPSIA information can be obtained
at www.ICGtesting.com
Printed in the USA
BVHW031927230623
666301BV00006B/346